Getting To Know...

Nature's Children

PELICANS

Candace Savage

SCHOLASTIC INC.

New York Toronto London Auckland Sydney
Mexico City New Delhi Hong Kong Buenos Aires

Facts in Brief

Classification of North American pelicans

Class: *Aves* (birds)
Order: *Pelecaniformes* (pelican-like birds)
Family: *Pelecanidae* (pelican family)
Genus: *Pelecanus* (pelican)
Species: *Pelecanus erythrorhynchos* (White Pelican)
        Pelecanus occidentalis (Brown Pelican)

World distribution. North and South America; closely related species are found in most parts of the world.

Habitat. Lakes, rivers, seashore.

Distinctive physical characteristics. Long pointed beak under which hangs a large throat pouch; large wingspan.

Habits. Nests in colonies; builds nest on the ground; travels in flocks, sometimes in a "V" formation.

Diet. Fish.

Published by Scholastic Inc.
90 Old Sherman Turnpike, Danbury, Connecticut 06816.

SCHOLASTIC and associated logos are trademarks of Scholastic Inc.

ISBN 0-7172-6705-9   Printed in the U.S.A.

Edited by: Elizabeth Grace Zuraw   *Photo Editor:* Nancy Norton
Photo Rights: Ivy Images   *Cover Design*: Niemand Design

Have you ever wondered . . .

Before you start reading about pelicans, here's a little fun project for you to do. Get a piece of paper and a pencil or color pens. Now draw a bird. Make it the strangest bird you can imagine, but don't forget to give it the basic bird features: a head, two eyes, a beak, a body, two wings, and two legs. Be sure to give it feathers, too. Otherwise your creation won't look like a bird.

When you've finished, compare your drawing of the imaginary bird with the pictures of pelicans in this book. Which is stranger, the real birds or your make-believe one? Or are they all more or less on the odd side? Or maybe you win, after all! Maybe your bird is the most bizarre and comical. But while you're deciding, remember this: Pelicans really do exist. They're not imaginary like your bird. Don't you think that makes the pelican the strangest-looking bird of all?

A pelican may look clumsy and hunchbacked while walking or sitting still, but it's a graceful flier and a superb swimmer.

A Pod of Pelicans

As soon as a young pelican can climb out of its nest, it looks for other pelicans its own age. At first, the youngsters just get together during the day, each returning to its own nest at night where one of its parents will keep it warm. But later on, the young birds spend all of their time in groups called *pods*.

The youngsters in these pods often do things together. They stay close together, just like flocks of sheep, and they're great imitators. If one bird moves to the shade, dozens follow. If one goes to the shore, a hundred others may tag along.

If they're frightened by a boat, a low-flying airplane, or a person, the young pelicans will rush together in a squirming, wriggling mass, sometimes crawling on top of one another as they all try to hide in the center of the pod.

Young White Pelicans squeeze together in a pod.

Pelicans Here and There

There are six different kinds of pelicans in the world today, with at least one kind on every continent. All pelicans are water birds and usually are found around rivers, lakes, and oceans.

In North America, there are two kinds of pelicans. The Brown Pelican lives on the ocean coasts of the southeastern and western United States. The White Pelican nests mostly on lakes in western Canada and the western United States.

One of the most obvious features of a pelican is its enormous beak.

Browns and Whites

It's easy to see how the two North American pelicans got their names—from the color of their *plumage,* or feathers. As you might expect, the Brown Pelican is mostly brown, but it has silvery gray streaks and white markings on the underside of its wings. The White Pelican is almost pure white, except for dark wingtips.

Both kinds of pelicans are easy to spot, whether they're in the air or in the water. They fly with their heads pulled back and their big beaks resting lightly on their chests. In the water they float high because of air trapped in their feathers and in *air sacs*—small pouches— under their skin.

This isn't a pelican gymnast rehearsing a routine! The bird is just preening, *or using its beak to clean and smooth its feathers.*

Two Homes

Pelicans that nest in northern areas, where winters are cold, often have two homes. In the fall, when chilly winds begin to blow and the temperature drops to near freezing, these pelicans leave their nesting grounds and head south in search of a friendlier climate.

Some pelicans must fly hundreds of miles (kilometers) between their summer nesting grounds and winter feeding grounds. The flight that birds make from one place to another in search of food and a suitable climate is called *migration*. Fortunately, pelicans are well equipped for long-distance flying.

The pelican's powerful wings can carry it through the air at speeds of more than 40 miles (25 kilometers) per hour.

Heavy Flyer

One of the most impressive things about pelicans is their size. They are among North America's largest birds.

Adult White Pelicans sometimes weigh more than 22 pounds (10 kilograms). That's about the same as a large turkey. Brown Pelicans are slightly smaller.

Because they're so heavy, pelicans often have to work hard to get airborne. They always take off into the wind. If there is no wind, they get up speed by running across the surface of the water, beating their wings and pumping their feet as they go. When they're finally moving fast enough, they rise into the air.

However graceful a pelican may be while in flight, there's nothing smooth about a pelican landing. The bird often just plops down with a splash, sometimes with its feet sticking out in front to act as brakes.

Because of the pelican's large size, liftoff and landing aren't this bird's most elegant moves.

Lots of Wing Power

Pelicans have a huge *wingspan*—the distance between the tips of a bird's extended wings. How big? To find out, take a ruler and measure 8 feet (2.5 meters) on the floor. That's how far an adult White Pelican's wings will reach when they're stretched out. Some pelicans' wingspans are even wider!

Once pelicans are in the air, they fly with grace and strength, thanks to their powerful wings. Sometimes they flap their wings; other times they glide on rising currents of warm air. When they glide, it seems magical to see their heavy bodies sailing, silent and motionless, through the sky. They can ride up on air currents, higher and higher, until they're no more than tiny specks to the human eye.

The ancestors of the pelicans we see today can be traced back about 100 million years to the age of the dinosaurs.

A Flock of Flyers

Pelicans usually fly in flocks. In fact, they do almost everything in flocks. Pelicans are very social birds—they like doing things together.

Often pelicans travel one behind the other in a long line. Sometimes they fly in a wide "V" formation. Their wing beats are very slow and dignified: flap, flap, flap, and g-l-i-d-e. Each bird takes its cue from the one in front of it, so that they either move their wings at the same time or one after the other. Often the flapping motion seems to pass down the line of pelicans like a wave.

Pelicans like togetherness. Not only do they fly in flocks, but even when a group is at rest on land, all the birds usually point their heads in the same direction!

Sky Fishers

Brown Pelicans fish from the sky—which actually isn't as strange as it sounds. What they do from high above is spot fish that are swimming just below the surface of the water. Then the pelicans dive headfirst into the ocean and catch the fish in their beaks. Usually the birds plunge down from a height of 23 feet (7 meters). And they plan their dives so carefully that they end up exactly where the fish are! Fortunately, crashing into the water at high speed from way up in the air doesn't hurt these birds. Air trapped in pockets under their skin and between their feathers helps to cushion the force of their dives.

Brown Pelicans catch small fish that live in schools, including pigfish, sheepshead, pinfish, and silversides.

A Brown Pelican dives for its meal.

The Brown Pelican has sharp eyesight to help it locate fish that swim just beneath the surface of the water.

Opposite page:
Pelicans have
hearty appetites.
A pelican can
sometimes eat up
to 8 pounds (3.5
kilograms) of
food a day.

Sly Fishers

White Pelicans are fish eaters, too, but unlike Brown Pelicans, they don't make spectacular dives to catch a meal. Instead, they dip their beaks—and often their heads—underwater as they swim and scoop up their food. They eat whatever is easiest to catch: minnows, perch, and carp, and sometimes frogs or salamanders.

When they're fishing in deep water, White Pelicans usually feed alone. But when they're in shallow waters, they often work together.

Here's how. A number of pelicans paddle around, not seeming to pay much attention to one another. But the instant a school of fish swims among them, the birds form a ring around the fish. The pelicans move in slowly, while beating the water with their wings to herd the fish toward the center of the ring. When the fish are packed together in the middle of the circle, the pelicans begin a genuine "feeding frenzy"—a wild free-for-all of jabbing beaks and splashing feet. Such a cooperative method of fishing enables each bird to get a bigger meal than it would if it were fishing alone.

A Handy Scoop Net

All pelicans have a special tool that they use for fishing. Can you guess what it might be?

If your answer is the bird's famous beak with its attached pouch, then you're quite right. The *pouch* is the large pocket on the underside of the pelican's beak. It's made of material that stretches like a balloon. A pelican's beak and pouch serve as a dip net. The pelican dips its beak into the water and scoops up a pouchful of water. If it's lucky, there'll be some fish in the trapped water, too. When its pouch is full, the pelican squeezes out the water and swallows the fish whole.

The pelican's pouch is so stretchy that it can hold from 2 to 3 gallons (7.6 to 11.4 liters) of water and fish. How much is that? To find out, put a stopper in your kitchen sink. Then get a one-quart (one-liter) milk carton, fill it with water, and empty it into the sink. Do that about ten times and you'll get a general idea of how much a pelican's pouch can hold.

Opposite page: *You may have heard the rhyme about the pelican, which says that its beak can hold more than its belican (belly can). That's true if you count the pelican's pouch, which has twice the capacity of its stomach!*

Big Mouth

You've probably seen cartoons that show pelicans flying and walking while holding different objects in their beaks. In real life, however, pelicans don't do this. Their beaks aren't made for carrying things.

If you put something in your pocket, you can be pretty sure it'll stay there because your pocket has a bottom. But a pelican's pouch is just a stretchy tube that empties into the bird's throat. As soon as the pelican lifts its head, any fish in its pouch slide down its throat into its stomach—and the pouch shrinks up.

Pelicans' throats and stomachs are stretchy, too. When the fishing is good, the birds stuff themselves to the very brim. They often eat several hundred minnows at a time. Sometimes they pack in so much food that they can't even get airborne! They have to throw back part of their catch in order to take off.

The pelican's enormous pouch may not be glamorous or dainty looking, but it's a perfect tool for catching fish.

Air-conditioned Pouches

Fishing isn't the only way that pelicans use their pouches. They also use them as a way of keeping cool. How?

Have you ever noticed a dog on a very hot day? What does it do with its tongue? It sticks it out and *pants,* or breathes fasts. When the dog pants, air moves over the moist surface of its tongue and the dog cools off. Try it yourself— but not in public! When you stick out your tongue and air passes over it, doesn't your tongue feel cool?

When a pelican is very hot, it opens its beak and flutters the moist skin of its pouch so that air moves around it. How do you think that makes its pouch feel?

It may not be as easy as turning a dial on an air conditioner and sitting back, but some quick flutters of the pouch can get a pelican welcome relief in hot weather.

Pelican Talk

Believe it or not, pelicans also use their pouches to help them communicate with each other.

When two White Pelicans meet, they sometimes puff out their pouches, point their beaks straight up, and turn their heads slowly from side to side. This is the pelicans' way of saying hello. Such greetings are important for pelicans because, unlike other birds, pelicans are usually silent. They don't communicate by making sounds—except for young pelicans. They can get quite noisy, especially at feeding time.

In spite of the huge size of the pelican's beak, it isn't used to make sounds.

Web-footed Friends

If you spent as much time in the water as a pelican does, you'd want to wear flippers to help you get around. A pelican doesn't need flippers. Its feet are *webbed*—the toes are joined together by flaps of skin. Such feet give the pelican paddling power aplenty.

Unfortunately, webbed feet aren't always a help. In fact, on land they can be a bit of a nuisance, as you'd know if you've ever tried walking in flippers. A pelican on land has to throw its body from side to side and waddle awkwardly. That's quite a change from its graceful, fast-speed swimming style.

Opposite page: *Its webbed feet make a pelican move clumsily on land, but just watch this bird's performance when it hits the water!*

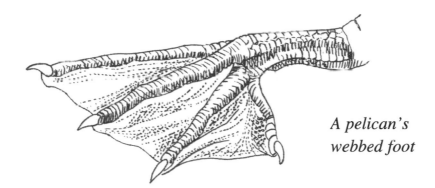

A pelican's webbed foot

Courting Time

Depending on where they live, Brown Pelicans *mate,* or come together to produce young, at various times during the year. White Pelicans mate in late spring. But before a pelican can mate, it must attract a partner.

As part of their *courtship*—the process of attracting a mate—pelicans perform a special dance. Though it's showy, it's not like any dance that people do. Sometimes a male pelican will stomp in a flat-footed way around a female. Other times the male will strut around and bow, as if to say, "Don't you think I'm handsome!"

Like many birds, White Pelicans put on their brightest colors to attract a mate. But they wear their bright colors on their pouches, not their feathers. For most of the year, a White Pelican's pouch is a dull yellow-orange, but in spring it turns bright orange. At the same time, the birds grow a *horn,* or bump, on their bills. *Ornithologists*—scientists who study birds—aren't sure why. White Pelicans also grow a pale yellow *crest,* or tuft of feathers, on their heads, and pale yellow chest feathers.

The horn on a White Pelican's beak can grow to a height of 4 inches (10 centimeters), but it's only temporary. It falls off after mating season.

Quite a Crowd

White Pelicans always make their nests on islands, usually far out in lakes. The remoteness of islands keeps their eggs away from people and safe from hungry *predators,* or animals that hunt other animals for food. Brown Pelicans often nest on islands, too, but they'll also choose other nest sites if they seem safe. If you come across a pelican nest, it's very important to stay away from it. By going close, you may upset the pelican parents and make them leave their nest. If that happens, the young pelicans die.

Pelicans don't nest alone, but rather, in *colonies,* or sites where hundreds of pelicans lay their eggs and raise their young. A pelican colony is a crowded—and messy—place. The ground is often covered with bird waste and rotting fish, so you can imagine how it smells!

Sometimes as many as a thousand pairs of pelicans may gather together in a colony.

Sticks and Stones

Both pelican parents help with nest building. The job is easy for White Pelicans. The birds simply sit on the ground and turn round and round, dragging their bills as they go. As they turn, the pelicans pull earth, twigs, and small stones into a saucer-like ring. Presto—a nest!

Brown Pelicans put a bit more work into building their nests. The pelican pair gathers sticks and makes a platform with a hollow in the middle for the eggs.

When the nest is ready, the mother pelican lays two or three eggs. For a whole month, the parents take turns sitting on the eggs. Like other birds, pelicans have to keep their eggs warm so that the young can grow inside.

For both Brown and White Pelican parents, egg-sitting is a joint venture. Mothers and fathers take turns at the job.

Is It a Bird?

When a baby pelican *hatches,* or breaks out of its egg, it doesn't even look like a bird. It looks more like a *reptile,* a class of animals that includes lizards, alligators, snakes, and turtles. The baby pelican is pink-skinned and featherless and so small and weak that it can scarcely raise its head. At feeding time, its parents dribble food into its tiny mouth from the tips of their huge beaks.

But come back to the nest a month later and you'll see a much different scene. The young pelican, called a *hatchling,* is now much bigger and covered in *down,* or soft, fluffy white feathers. And the baby can walk, though in a teetering, tottering, toddler sort of way, tripping over nothing and often falling down.

In appearance, pelican hatchlings can easily rival the ugliest of ducklings.

A Hungry Horde

Opposite page:
Pelican parents will feed only their own young. No one knows how the parents recognize their own babies amid the mass of loud clamoring chicks, but they do. The young recognize their parents, too.

Young pelicans leave the nest and join a pod of other youngsters before they're able to fly or feed themselves. But their parents return to feed the young birds several times a day. It's a big job. A young pelican eats about 150 pounds (70 kilograms) of fish—and that's before it has even left its nest to join a pod!

When an adult arrives with food, the young pelicans act as if they're starving to death. They peck at the adult's feet, reach for its beak, and even climb up its body. Some of the little birds appear to go crazy: They fling themselves on the ground, flap wildly, and wave their heads back and forth. Or they twirl round and round, growling and biting their wings. It's their way of saying, "Feed me!"

Would you like to dine by reaching into your parent's throat for some half-digested fish? Probably not, but that's how young pelicans feed. Often they refuse to remove their heads from the parent's throat when the adult wants to leave. The youngsters actually have to be shaken loose by the trapped parent!

Learning to fly can be an awkward process for young pelicans, but as adults these birds are strong flyers. Some kinds of pelicans can stay in the air for hours.

First Flight

By the time they're about three months old, young pelicans are ready to *fledge,* or start flying. Take-offs and landings are especially difficult at first. The young birds awkwardly blunder up into the air and then belly flop into the water. But practice makes perfect, and soon they're flying confidently. By the fall, young pelicans that live in cold climates are strong enough to join the adults on the long flight south to their winter feeding grounds.

The young pelicans don't get their full adult plumage until they're a year old. Then they look just like their parents. But although they *look* grown-up, they're not yet ready to have babies of their own. That won't happen until they're three or four years old. Still, many years will remain to raise families. In the wild, pelicans commonly survive 15 to 25 years.

A Helping Hand

Pelicans have faced many challenges from people and the world around them. *Pesticides*—chemicals used to kill insects—and other poisons sometimes wash from the land into the sea. Fish take in the poisons and then are eaten by pelicans who become sick or die or unable to lay healthy eggs.

Pelicans lose their *habitats,* or places where they live, when people move into wild areas once occupied by pelicans. And people sometimes over fish lakes and seas, leaving fewer fish for pelicans to eat. People's boats, too, disturb pelican nesting sites, and often pelicans get tangled in fishing nets and fishhooks.

But some people have been concerned about the pelican. When the pelican populations decreased greatly, the bird was declared an *endangered species,* an animal threatened with extinction. As a result, laws were passed banning certain pesticides, and wildlife refuges have been created to protect pelican habitats. If people continue to care about pelicans, these remarkable birds will remain an important and beautiful part of our natural world.

Words To Know

Colony   A nesting site where pelicans lay eggs and raise young.

Courtship   The process of attracting a mate.

Crest   A tuft of feathers on a bird's head.

Down   Very soft, fluffy feathers.

Endangered Species   Animals threatened with dying out.

Extinct   Having died out completely.

Fledge   To make a first flight.

Habitat   An area or type of area an animal or plant lives in.

Hatch   To break out of an egg.

Hatchling   A young bird.

Horn   A bump on a pelican's beak, appearing in mating season.

Mate   To come together to produce young.

Migration   Traveling at regular times of the year in search of food, a suitable climate, or a place to mate and raise young.

Ornithologist   A scientist who studies birds.

Pesticide   A chemical used to kill insects.

Plumage   The covering of feathers on a bird.

Pod   A group of young pelicans.

Pouch   The large pocket on the underside of a pelican's beak.

Predator   An animal that hunts other animals for food.

Preen   To use the beak to clean, smooth, and rearrange the feathers.

Reptiles   The class of animals that includes lizards, snakes, turtles, alligators, and crocodiles.

Webbed feet   Feet on which the toes are joined by flaps of skin.

Wingspan   The distance across a bird's fully extended wings.

Index

PHOTO CREDITS
Cover: A. Kerstitch, *Visuals Unlimited.* **Interiors:** J. D. Taylor, 4. /*Ivy Images:* Dr. George K. Peck, 7; Don Johnston, 27; Robert McCaw, 36; Alan & Sandy Carey, 43. /*Thomas Stack & Associates:* Mark A. Stack, 8. /*Valan Photos:* Stephen J. Krasemann, 11, 23, 30-31; Wayne Lankinen, 12, 16, 24, 32, 39; Dennis Schmidt, 18-19. /*Wayne Lankinen,* 15, 44. /*George Peck,* 20, 28, 40. /*Visuals Unlimited:* Charlie Heidecker, 35.

Getting To Know...

Nature's Children

SNAKES

Merebeth Switzer
and
Katherine Grier

SCHOLASTIC INC.

New York   Toronto   London   Auckland   Sydney
Mexico City   New Delhi   Hong Kong   Buenos Aires

Facts in Brief

Classification of North American snakes

Class: *Reptilia* (reptiles)

Order: *Ophidia* (snakes)

Family: 5 families of snakes in North America

Genus: 50 genera of snakes in North America

Species: Approximately 320 species and subspecies found in North America

World distribution.   Varies with species.

Habitat.   Varies with species.

Distinctive physical characteristics.   Long slim limbless body covered with dry scales; no external ears.

Habits.   Vary with species.

Diet.   All species are meat-eaters.

Published by Scholastic Inc.
90 Old Sherman Turnpike, Danbury, Connecticut 06816.

ISBN 0-7172-6705-9   Printed in the U.S.A.

Edited by: Elizabeth Grace Zuraw   *Photo Editor:* Nancy Norton
Photo Rights: Ivy Images   *Cover Design*: Niemand Design

Have you ever wondered . . .

When you see a snake gliding through the grass or basking on a warm rock, what's your reaction? People sometimes have strong feelings about snakes, and fear is one of those feelings. Snakes often are portrayed as villains. But there also have been many positive stories told about this much-berated creature.

The ancient Greeks, for example, were aware that snakes shed their old worn skins to reveal fine new skin underneath. The Greeks viewed this fresh new skin as a sign of renewed life and health. To this day, doctors use a picture of two snakes curling up a staff as a symbol for their profession.

One thing is certain: Snakes have been misunderstood. What are snakes really like? Only careful observation will tell. You can begin by reading and going outdoors or to natural history museums where you can see snakes. And scientists can tell us much about how snakes are suited for the role they play in the natural world. For now, just turn the page to learn some fascinating facts about this mysterious and maligned animal.

Opposite page: *Snakes live on every continent but Antarctica and in just about every kind of climate and terrain.*

Scaly Relatives

Lizards, turtles, alligators, and crocodiles are relatives of the snake. They all are *reptiles.* That means they're covered with tough, dry *scales*, or thin overlapping plates. Reptiles also breathe air into lungs, and their young usually hatch from eggs. And reptiles have no built-in temperature control. They're *cold-blooded*—their body temperature is affected by their surroundings. In these ways, all reptiles are alike.

But in other ways, snakes are not like their reptile relatives. One big difference is easy to see. Snakes don't have legs. A few still have small bones and a claw left where their ancestors had hip and leg bones, but these leg leftovers don't help the snake move.

Why don't snakes have legs? Scientists believe that long ago, the snake's lizard-like ancestors began to hunt for food in other animals' *burrows,* or underground homes. But their legs got in the way in the narrow spaces. Gradually their legs disappeared so that snakes could hunt more successfully underground.

A young copperhead's tail is a handy tool for catching a meal. The tail has a distinctive yellow tip that the copperhead can wave back and forth to attract mice or other small animals.

Snakes, Snakes, and More Snakes

About 320 different kinds of snakes live in North America. They all need food, water, warmth, and shelter to survive. They find these basics in many different kinds of places. Some snakes live in deserts, while others live in forests, mountains, or grasslands. Some spend much of their time burrowing underground, and others live almost entirely above ground. There are snakes almost everywhere in North America and the rest of the world, except in the far north where the winters are very long and cold. There are no snakes around the North and South Poles or on the top of high mountain ranges.

The beautiful Smooth Green Snake is rarely seen because it blends in so well with the surrounding greenery.

Long and Slim

Opposite page: *Occasionally snakes are born all black instead of their regular color. This Garter Snake is hard to recognize without its stripes. Garter Snakes, the most common snakes in North America, usually have some pattern of three stripes running down their bodies.*

Some snakes are huge. The largest snakes in the world can grow to the length of five men lying head to toe. But in North America, the largest snakes grow only as long as a man is tall. The shortest is about the length of a new pencil. Most are somewhere in between.

Big or small, a snake's body shape is the same—long and slim. The snake has many of the same kinds of organs as you do, and the organs do the same sorts of jobs: breathe in air, pump and clean the blood, take in nourishment from food, and get rid of waste materials.

But how do all the organs fit in a snake? The organs themselves are long and slim just like the snake's body, and they're arranged a little differently than they are in other animals' bodies. In most snakes, if there once were two organs of one kind—lungs, for example—one has either shrunk or disappeared completely, leaving just one to do the work of two.

A snake's eyes, like those of this Yellow-bellied Racer, are protected by an outer layer of skin instead of by eyelids that open and close. That's why a snake's eyes are always open, even when it's asleep.

A Skin of Scales

A snake's skin is made up of many scales.
There are small scales on its back and sides
and larger ones on its head. Running from
head to tail along its belly is a row of big
rectangular scales called *scutes.*

A snake's scales look like separate pieces
of skin, but they're not. The snake's outer skin
is all one piece. In between the scales, there
are hidden folds of skin that join each scale to
the next one. These folds allow the snake's
skin to stretch as the reptile curves its body or
swallows a large meal.

A snake has three layers of skin. The inner
layer holds the snake's colors and patterns.
The middle layer is like a factory, continually
producing the cells that make up the outer
layer. The outer layer, which is transparent,
hard, and thin, is made of *keratin,* the same
substance your hair and fingernails are made
of. The outer layer protects the snake from
rough objects as it moves along the ground.
This outer skin even covers the snake's eyes
like a clear bubble.

Changing Skins

Opposite page:
This Eastern Milk Snake is about to shed its skin. Note its foggy eye, as the old skin on the eye loosens.

Garter Snake shedding its skin.

You lose tiny flakes of old skin every day, but a snake sheds its old outer skin all in one piece. Shedding its skin is important for a snake.

Young snakes need room for their growing bodies, but their outer skins never grow. So they must grow new, larger skins—sometimes up to six times a year. Older snakes don't grow as fast, but their skins get worn with use, so they shed once or twice a year. A baby snake may shed its first skin at the age of two weeks.

A snake's old skin must separate from the new one before it can be shed. A milky liquid builds up under the outer skin and loosens it. It even covers the snake's eyes so that the animal can't see very well. A few days later the snake rubs its nose against a twig and makes a break in the old skin. Then it slithers out of the skin, peeling it off inside out just as you would pull a sweater over your head.

The old skin is clear but it shows the outline of every scale and all the folds of skin in between. The new skin is shiny, and shows the snake's colors and patterns brightly.

No Arms or Legs, But Can They Move

Think for a moment of the parts of your body that you use when you walk, run, or swim. It's hard to imagine moving without arms and legs, isn't it? But a snake doesn't have arms or legs—or fins or wings. How, then, can it move so easily and gracefully?

The snake has a backbone that runs from the base of its head to the tip of its tail. This backbone is made up of many small bones that are all connected. Each bone can move slightly sideways and up and down, enabling the snake to curve back and forth.

But a snake's bones couldn't go anywhere without the muscles that are attached to them. A snake moves by tightening or relaxing its muscles, just as you do. The muscles pull or push the bones so that the snake's whole body moves forward, backward, or sideways. To help move itself along, the snake grabs onto twigs or rocks or bark with its scutes. They give the snake a good grip and keep it from slipping backward.

Opposite page: The cottonmouth, which grows more than three feet in length, lives in the swamps and wetlands of the southern United States.

17

Different Places, Different Moves

Just as you can, a snake is able to move in several different ways. It can curve its body into an S and wriggle forward. In water or on land, this is the way most snakes travel.

Or a snake can move by sidewinding. The snake curves its body into S-shaped loops and throws each loop sideways, clear of the ground. Snakes use this method in shifting sand where scutes can't get a good grip. And because only the bends of each loop—and not the head and neck—land on the ground, many snakes use sidewinding if they're moving across hot sand.

A snake can also push and pull itself up trees or along narrow passages. First it folds the front half of its body into tight loops, somewhat like an accordion, gripping with its front scutes. Next, as it straightens the front part of its body, it pulls the back half of its body forward into new loops, and takes hold with its rear scutes. Then it begins all over again.

Opposite page:
The Milk Snake got its name because farmers once believed that the snake took milk from their cows. But that's not true. When a Milk Snake goes into a barn, it's only to hunt for mice or rats.

Finally, a snake can creep along in an almost straight line. For a long, heavy snake, this is much easier than weaving from side to side. Its muscles lift and pull a scute ahead. The scute grips the ground where it lands. The muscles move the next scute ahead and the next and the next. The muscles pull the snake's body forward bit by bit.

Most snakes have their own favorite way of moving, such as sidewinding. But many use a combination of moves. For example, a heavy snake that usually creeps forward in a straight line can use the wavy S movement if it needs to move fast.

You might think that snakes move easily only on land, but most snakes can also swim if they have to. And some water snakes hunt for food in the shallows of lakes and rivers and swim long distances across open water.

Even though a water snake spends a great deal of time searching for food in ponds and lakes, it sleeps on dry ground.

Snake Sense

You learn about your world by seeing, hearing, touching, smelling, and tasting it. Snakes learn about their world a little differently.

Snakes' eyes and ears don't work the way yours do. They can't see very clearly or tell how far away things are. And snakes don't have ears like yours with eardrums that pick up sounds carried by air. When a snake charmer plays a flute, the snake doesn't hear a sound. It sways to the charmer's movements.

A snake's sense of touch is more like yours. Although its skin is scaly, it can feel all over. And many snakes that hunt warm-blooded animals have special organs known as *heat sensors*—sensitive holes on the snake's snout. The sensors tell the snake if something warm—and maybe good to eat—is nearby. The holes, also called *pits,* are especially well developed in a group of snakes called *pit vipers.* The name *viper* is given to any one of a group of poisonous snakes.

Opposite page:
Rattlesnakes and copperheads, such as the one shown here, are pit vipers.

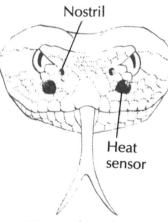

Nostril

Heat sensor

Using their heat sensors, some snakes can hunt and strike in total darkness. The sensors can detect tiny changes in temperature and can easily pinpoint the exact location of prey.

A Tongue With a Difference

Although a snake learns a lot about its world through vibration and touch, it learns most by using its tongue. A snake's tongue is long and forked at the end. The tongue can hardly taste things at all, but it *can* smell things. How?

If you watch a snake you'll see that it's always darting its tongue in and out if its mouth. The tongue picks up tiny bits of scent information from the air and the ground. When the snake pulls its tongue back into its mouth, it puts the forked tips into two small openings in the roof of its mouth. These openings work just like your nose. They send signals to the snake's brain to tell it what it has "smelled" with its tongue.

You use your tongue primarily for its sense of taste. Not so with snakes. A snake uses its tongue for smelling.

Skilled Hunters

All snakes are meat eaters. But they catch their *prey*—an animal hunted by another animal for food—in different ways. Some catch and hold their prey with their teeth before eating it live. Some snakes are *constrictors*—they coil around their prey and squeeze it so it can't breathe. And other snakes poison their catch by spurting *venom,* or poison, into the prey through long hollow teeth called *fangs.* The venom is made in a small gland at the back of the snake's mouth. A *gland* is a part of an animal's body that makes and gives out a substance.

Once a snake has caught its prey, it eats it whole. It can't do anything else. It doesn't have sharp cutting teeth or flat chewing teeth. Its teeth are pointy and curved inward, good only for holding onto its prey.

Depending on a snake's size, it eats insects, frogs, mice, rats, snakes, larger animals, or the remains of other hunters' kills. It can swallow a meal several times bigger than its mouth.

A snake's fangs swing outward when the snake attacks, and pull back into their sheaths, *or coverings, when the snake closes its mouth.*

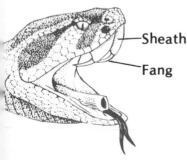

Sheath

Fang

This Pacific Rattlesnake has taken over a bird's nest.

*A cottonmouth, shown here swallowing a fish, gets
its name from the white lining in its mouth.*

Super Swallowers

Imagine trying to swallow an apple whole. Could you do it? Of course not! So how can a snake swallow something larger than its own head?

To a snake, big mouthfuls aren't a problem. Its jawbones can detach from the rest of its skull and from each other to stretch open. The bottom jawbones even split in the middle. That gives the snake a huge mouth and no bones to get in the way.

But even with such a big mouth, swallowing is a slow business. Bit by bit, the snake works its jaws around its prey. Then its throat starts to tighten and pull the animal into the snake's stomach. Before long there's no sign of the prey—except for a bulge moving slowly down the snake's body.

A snake that has swallowed a big meal may take days or even weeks to digest all of it. During that time it won't need to eat anything else.

Avoiding Danger

Snakes have many enemies in the natural world—meat-eating birds and animals and other reptiles, including snakes.

Some snakes use *camouflage,* or blending in with their surroundings, to help them hide from their enemies. For example, it's difficult to see a green snake among leaves or grass, or a mottled black and brown snake among rocks or sand. Other snakes are brightly colored—and often also are very poisonous. Some *herpetologists*—scientists who study snakes and other reptiles—believe that a snake's bright colors warn its enemies that it's dangerous.

When a snake senses danger, the first thing it does is try to get away. If it can't flee, it tries to protect itself.

Ring-necked Snakes have tails with a brightly colored underside that stays hidden when the snake is at rest. When threatened, the snake flashes the color to startle an enemy.

Defense Tactics

Some kinds of snakes try to scare their enemies away. They hiss or rattle their tails or puff themselves up so that they look big and ferocious. Others give off a *musk*—a strong, smelly, terrible tasting substance—if they're picked up. And some even roll over and play dead!

A few snakes are quick to attack. But most strike only if they can't escape or scare off their enemies. The weapons they use to defend themselves are the same ones they use for hunting. Some bite, some use venom, and some try to squeeze their enemies so they can't breathe.

A rattlesnake's tail has several horny rings that rattle against each other when the snake shakes or vibrates the tail. The sound is a warning not to be ignored: "Back off!"

Too Hot? Too Cold?

You are *warm-blooded*. This means that your body temperature stays much the same no matter how hot or cold the weather is.

Because snakes are cold-blooded, their bodies don't control their temperature as ours do. If it gets cold out, the snake's body temperature drops. If it gets hot, the snake's temperature rises. But snakes like the same range of temperature that most of us do—T-shirt weather. That's when their bodies work best, enabling them to be alert and agile.

A snake must control its temperature by moving to places where it's warmer or cooler, depending on its needs. A snake warms itself by basking in the sun out of the wind. It can cool itself by seeking shade or wet shorelines or by going underground.

Big snakes don't live in cool climates. It would be too hard for them to keep warm. Many snakes that do live where it's cooler are brown or black. Their dark colors take in the sun's warmth much faster than lighter colors would and help them keep warm.

Opposite page:
The Small Brown or DeKay's Snake is just that—small. Often it doesn't grow longer than about 12 inches (30 centimeters).

Overleaf:
The Hog-nosed Snake may open its mouth wide and hiss, but it has never been known to bite.

35

Away from Winter's Chill

How do snakes in cold-weather country survive winter? As the days grow shorter and colder, snakes move more slowly and become less alert. When it's too chilly for them to warm themselves in the sun, they have to look for shelter. They need protection from freezing weather and warm-blooded enemies.

A snake's winter shelter is called the snake's *hibernaculum.* It can be a crevice in rocks, a space under a log, or an animal's burrow. In very cold areas, the shelter needs to be deep underground, safely below the frost line.

Once the snake has found shelter, it *hibernates*, or goes into a kind of deep sleep, for the whole winter. Its heart beats more slowly, and it breathes less often. And because it stays still, it uses so little energy that it doesn't need to eat again until spring.

Some snakes hibernate alone, but a large hole or burrow can attract many snakes. Different kinds of snake and sometimes even enemies pass the winter side by side. A snake returns to the same shelter year after year.

Opposite page:
As winter approaches, a cluster of rattle-snakes in a cold northern region will trade a sunny open-air perch for a deep, protected hibernaculum.

39

Spring Mating

As the spring days grow warmer and longer, snakes that have spent the winter hibernating wriggle out of their shelters. The warm weather tells them that now is the time to *mate,* or come together to produce young. The male finds a female by following the scent she leaves on the ground. Snakes often mate with different partners during mating season.

Sometimes two males confront each other to determine which one will mate with a female. The males lift their heads, twist their bodies together, and try to upset each other's balance. But they don't bite or hiss. Eventually the weaker snake leaves, and the stronger one gets to mate with the female.

Garter Snakes often mate in large groups. Here two males, who usually are smaller in size than the females, try to attract a female.

A New Year, New Babies

Baby snakes start their lives in different ways. Some are born from eggs, while others are born live. With some egg-laying snakes, the mother finds a warm, safe place to lay her eggs—perhaps in a rotting log or a burrow or under leaves. Some kinds of snakes lay as few as 7 eggs while others lay as many as 60.

The eggs are white, but the shells aren't brittle like chicken eggs. Instead, they feel like Ping-Pong balls, only a little softer. Inside each egg, a baby snake feeds on the yolk. When the baby is ready to *hatch,* or break out of its shell, it uses a small, sharp egg tooth to chip its way through the shell. An *egg tooth* is a hard point on the tip of a baby snake's nose. Soon after the egg tooth's work is done, it drops off the baby's nose.

This Eastern Hog-nosed Snake hatchling will grow up to be a great actor. When threatened, it'll turn on its back and writhe as if in pain. Then, with tongue hanging out, it will play dead—until the intruder leaves.

The babies of some other egg-laying snakes live inside the eggs that their mother carries inside her body until the time that they're ready to hatch. These babies also live on their egg's yolk. But the shells of their eggs are thin and they break open as they're pushed from their mother's body. They don't wait to hatch at a later time.

And finally, some baby snakes are born live. They live inside a clear *sac,* or pouch-like structure, inside their mother's body. After they're born, the baby snakes' first job is to break out of the sac.

The Eastern Milk Snake, like all milk snakes, is not poisonous, but some milk snakes look like snakes that are. If you're ever bitten by any kind of snake, get medical attention immediately.

A Hard Start

Life is dangerous for a baby snake. Its mother leaves as soon as she lays her eggs or her babies are born. Many eggs and babies become food for *predators*—animals that hunt other animals for food. Still, many young snakes do survive.

Baby snakes are like their parents in every way but size. For their first few years, they grow quickly. In places where the weather is warm all year, young snakes grow all year. Snakes that hibernate don't grow during winter, but they grow extra fast once the warm weather returns. In fact, snakes never really stop growing, although older snakes grow so slowly that you'd hardly notice it.

Herpetologists don't know how long snakes live in the wild. But they can guess because they've watched snakes in captivity. There, large snakes often live for more than 20 years, and smaller ones often live to be 10 or 15 years of age.

Words To Know

Burrow   A hole dug in the ground by an animal for use as a home.

Camouflage   Animal features that blend in with its surroundings.

Cold-blooded   Having a body temperature that's controlled by the temperature of the surrounding air or water. When an animal is warm-blooded, its temperature stays about the same all the time.

Constrictor   A snake that kills prey by squeezing it so it can't breathe.

Egg tooth   A point on a baby snake's nose, for breaking out of its shell.

Fangs   Long, sharp, hollow teeth through which venom flows.

Gland   A part of an animal's body that makes and gives out a substance.

Hatch   To break out of an egg.

Heat sensors   Organs that are specially sensitive to temperature.

Herpetologist   A scientist that studies snakes and other reptiles.

Hibernaculum   Place where a snake or group of snakes hibernates.

Hibernate   To go into a kind of long, deep sleep for the entire winter.

Mate   To come together to produce young.

Musk   A strong smelling substance produced by some animals.

Pit Viper   A poisonous snake that has heat sensing pits on it snout.

Predator   An animal that hunts other animals for food.

Prey   An animal hunted by another animal for food.

Reptiles   Class of cold-blooded animals that breathe air into lungs, usually hatch from eggs, and are covered with tough dry scales.

Scales   Thin, hard, overlapping plates that protect a snake's skin.

Scutes   The big rectangular scales on a snake's body.

Venom   The poisonous fluid produced by some snakes.

Viper   Any of a group of poisonous snakes having fangs.

Index